Oh Come All Ye Tasteful

The Foodie's Guide to a

Millionaire's Christmas Feast

by Ian Flitcroft

Paperbooks Ltd
175-185 Gray's Inn Road, London, WC1X 8UE
info@legend-paperbooks.co.uk | www.legendpress.co.uk

Contents © Ian Flitcroft 2015

Print ISBN 978-1-9102663-2-8
Ebook ISBN 978-1-9102663-3-5

Set in Times. Printed in the United Kingdom by Clays Ltd.
Cover design and illustrations by Kate Forrester www.kateforrester.co.uk

Oh Come All Ye Tasteful
Joyful and Triumphant,
Oh Come Ye, Oh Come Ye,
to Dine Here Well.

Table of Contents

Introduction

For the unprepared, Christmas lunch can be a veritable minefield. Like the Noel-tide truce in Ypres during World War I, this meal is often both surreal and dangerous. Murderous in-laws glare at you across the no-man's land of the dining table, their machine guns hidden within their sleeves. One stray word might be enough to set off World War III. Though one can usually choose a husband or wife, it is doubtful you'd select all, or any, of the motley collection of relatives that gather in your home at this time of year. As well as the same faces, Christmas lunch is made worse by the woeful lack of variety on the plate. This is, needless to say, a recipe for the total disaster that often ensues.

Since you're stuck with your family, the only solution is to become creative when it comes to what is served up.

What's that you say? A turkey is a turkey? Of course it is, but that dry over-cooked bird will soar when stuffed with pigeon breast, foie gras, black truffles and a few ortolan. And besides the turkey, there are a wide range of our feathered friends who can more than rise to the challenge of a Christmas fowl.

So fear not, this book will help you create a Christmas dinner that is so wildly impressive that even the most curmudgeonly great aunt will swoon. As well as tasting sublime, the food will be so comment-worthy that you'll be able to get through the whole meal talking entirely about the food. So all the usual incendiary topics that might rear their heads, from football to the sexual mores of the younger members of the family, will be duly banished.

There will be peace in the dining room, even if the kitchen and your bank balance have been destroyed in the process.

Trust me, it will be worth it!

The Perfect Christmas Lunch

What makes for a perfect Christmas lunch? There may be quite a few of you who think that tradition is the most important ingredient. To counter that let me just say that tradition, like socks, can wear thin; especially if you receive them as gifts every year. So I'll concede tradition is important, but it's not the most important aspect of this meal. To transform your Christmas dining you need to let go of a few of your treasured traditions. This book will show you how to replace your boiled-to-death, once-a-year sprouts with gastronomic traditions from the past that are worth bringing back, and new ideas from the present, so all your future Christmases will be bright and merry. Did you spot the Dickens reference there? I do hope so, because there are several Dickensian-era traditions in this book that will help to get your Christmas off to a fine start.

Heaped up on the floor, to form a kind of throne, were turkeys, geese, game, poultry, brawn, great joints of meat, sucking-pigs, long wreaths of sausages, mince-pies, plum-puddings, barrels of oysters, red-hot chestnuts, cherry-cheeked apples, juicy oranges, luscious pears, immense twelfth-cakes, and seething bowls of punch, that made the chamber dim with their delicious steam…
Charles Dickens, *A Christmas Carol* (1843)

What are the other ingredients of the perfect Christmas lunch? Top of the list has to be *extravagance*. This isn't just a meal, it is a feast; the nearest most of us will ever get to that Henry the Eighth-style banquet with roast swans on silver platters and Irish wolfhounds slouching around waiting for a half-chewed leg of lamb to be thrown over someone's shoulder. This feasting heritage goes all the way back to the pagan festivals of the winter solstice such as the Roman Saturnalia. This Roman holiday started on December 17th and ran until December 23rd when gifts were given. Sound familiar? While we may not share the Roman fondness for fried dormice and nightingales' tongues, there is no doubt that some Christmas traditions are decidedly unchristian.

••

Next on my list comes *taste*. Christmas fare should excite the palate and leave your taste buds jangling. Much as we all love Christmas lunch, the sense of occasion usually beats the taste. When was the last time you had a truly amazing gustatory experience at Christmas? This is a tragedy and one which this book will help to solve. As well as taste, Christmas lunch must also be a feast for the eyes. Those roast potatoes should sparkle. The turkey (or other fowl) should have the perfect hue and the table should be hidden under platefuls of every imaginable colour. The burning flames of brandy on the Christmas pudding should be dramatic (I'll explain a neat trick for that), not the usual anaemic blue that is almost invisible even with the lights out. Our eyes, along with our noses, are indeed another part of our sense of taste and are essential to capture the sense of theatre from a great meal.

After taste I would put *novelty* on the list of essential ingredients, though it is one that is often in short supply. Imagine if, every year, all the presents under the tree were the same. The first year would, of course, be fine. The second year the whole present concept would be beginning to lose its shine and five years later you'd all be sick of seeing the same random collection of golf gadgets, books and bath salts. So why should you do that with Christmas food? Wouldn't a few novel flavours and dishes spice up the whole affair? Of course it would. Even if you are determined to stick with turkey, you can liven up that old culinary chestnut with some spectacular additions.

....

Surprise is novelty's twin sister, but they are not identical twins. Novelty in food is usually something that you can see. A truly surprising food catches you off-guard. You might be expecting something entirely different, tricked by your eyes. Or the taste alone might be enough. We are often left to rely on Christmas crackers to provide both novelties and surprises (as well as dire jokes), but why not throw a few surprises onto the menu? Another twist that can spice up a Christmas lunch is devilment. Depending on your guest list and your own sense of humour you might consider playing a few tricks on your guests by serving up some really unusual treats – like chocolate-covered Brussels sprouts with the coffee!

....

As a small, and rather more serious aside, let us not forget *charity* as the last important ingredient of our Christmas celebrations.

Most of us are blessed with never having to ever experience true hunger. Let me make a suggestion. I'm sure you've come across the notion of off-setting your carbon emissions by donating to schemes where a tree is planted to assuage your guilt about catching a plane halfway across the world. But consider that as well as a carbon footprint, we also have a calorie footprint. If each of us set off the calories we consumed at Christmas and donated enough money for a similar amount of calories to be delivered to those around the world who truly need them, we would be making a small but valuable contribution to those in greatest need.

••

Don't be alarmed that everything in this book will be hard to make. The ingredients may be unusual, difficult to find and (at times) wildly expensive but the preparation is simple enough. Christmas is too short a day to spend it in the kitchen. I, like you, am a food enthusiast not a professional chef. To mangle a line from T.S. Eliot, "No! I am not Prince Heston, nor was meant to be". But now, as the Roman emperors used to say in the Colosseum,

Let the Games Commence!

Aperitifs, Cocktails & Wines

❝ Wine is bottled poetry.

Robert Louis Stevenson, *The Silverado Squatters*, 1884

Christmas and drinking go together like holly and ivy. Many of us, excepting the noble tribe of abstainers, will have over-indulged in all manner of alcoholic beverages at this time of year and suffered the consequences. So taking inspiration from Robert Louis Stevenson's book, I suggest that it is time to rethink your approach to alcohol.

Every true foodie should lean towards a gastronomical rather than a gluttonous approach to drink. This means that rather than drinking a firkin[1] of the same boring beer or supermarket wine, you should devote as much thought and consideration to what you drink as you do to what you eat. As well as adding surprising new tastes and novel twists, the bibulous aspects of Christmas are an area where you can display your extravagance to its greatest advantage. There are practical limits on how much you can spend on food at Christmas, but when it comes to spirits and wine you can easily sip your way through a king's ransom if you want to. If through some misfortune, entirely not of your making, you find yourself lacking the financial resources of a Russian oligarch, don't fret. There are plenty of ways of making a splash when it comes to Christmas drinks without having to fill your swimming pool with champagne and jumping in.

---

[1] An old English unit that equates to 9 gallons. This is, of course, an implausible volume to consume, but it is a wonderful-sounding word so I claim the defence of poetic licence in using it.

Aperitifs

Champagne is the definitive Christmas aperitif. It has an associated glamour that no other wine can match, despite its humble origins.

There was a time 800 years ago when the Champagne region was known more for its wool than its wine. To encourage people to buy their produce, merchants started giving out the flat, pinky-brown wine for free with every purchase of wool. It didn't start to become the drink we know today until a dedicated monk by the name of Dom Pierre Perignon, abbot of a Benedictine Abbey in Hautvillers, worked out in 1670 how to make a pure white wine from the red pinot grapes usually used in Champagne production. Back then the characteristic bubbles of champagne were thought to be a sign of a bad wine, but King Louis XIV and later his nephew Philippe II, Duke of Orléans, developed a taste for bubbles and introduced sparkling champagne into French high society. The rest is, of course, history.

Three Champagnes
that should impress your guests
(if not your accountant)

Cristal Champagne 2002 Vintage, by Louis Roederer

This champagne has the greatest bling factor, and is now inextricably linked with hip-hop. It is satisfyingly expensive (around £150 a bottle for the 2002, one of the best vintages of recent years) and epitomises the very newest of the nouveau riche. It is undoubtedly a very fine champagne, but I confess I wasn't totally blown away when I tried it. So why on earth serve it at Christmas? Well if Puff Daddy or Jay-Z are gathering around your table, it would be almost rude to serve anything else.

Krug Brut Grande Cuvée MV, David Sugar Engraved "Quail Design in Flowering Tree"

If you thought the Cristal was a touch pricey, then this little beauty might take you by surprise. The bottle, as you might guess from its name, is graced by an engraving of a quail in a flowering tree. What you might not guess is that it is also graced by a price tag of around £1000. Depending on your desire to impress, you might be tempted to leave the price tag on this one.

One of this champagne's claims to fame is that while the world's financial system was starting to grind to a halt during 2008, the value of a bottle of this champagne shot up from £900 to over £1300. It is clearly the first choice of those fortunate few who, when the banks crash, can just sigh languidly and reach for the Krug.

As expensive as the previous champagnes might be, they are mere drops in the ocean compared to the prices that have been paid recently for bottles of vintage champagne recovered from shipwrecks.

A few years ago a shipment of champagne was recovered from a schooner that sank off the Finnish archipelago of Åland. The boat sank sometime around 1830 and 162 bottles of champagne from the finest producers were recovered from the wreck. They were opened to see if they were drinkable and the seventy-nine bottles that passed the test were recorked for sale. While champagne can last a surprisingly long time in the bottle, this haul was undoubtedly helped by the cool dark conditions at the bottom of the sea. A year later in 2011, a bottle of Veuve Cliquot champagne from this wreck was sold for a world record price of €30,000 (£26,700 at the exchange rate at the time).

The bottles from this shipwreck certainly looked a little rough too, so an alternative and cheaper ploy might be to cellar your champagne in the bottom of the garden pond for a year and spin a mighty yarn about its watery origins when Christmas comes around again.

Mulled Wine - Smoking Bishop

While not quite an aperitif, mulled wine is a perfect start to any Christmas celebration, at any time of day or night.

Talking of which, I am old enough to remember a time when mulling wine still involved some effort and the use of some real ingredients. These days your local supermarket will provide a very decent screw top offering that can be poured straight into a saucepan or even microwaved in the glass (*quelle horreur*).

Even if embellished with a slice of orange these commercial offerings sum up everything that is wrong with a modern Christmas – too much commerce, and too little care.

So let's go back to basics and start with a recipe for mulled wine that goes back to Dickens' time and before – Smoking Bishop. But be warned! It is such a good drink that you might get carried away, like the reformed Mr Scrooge, and start giving away your millions to your struggling extended family.

To upgrade from a Bishop to an Archbishop use a decent claret. For a Cardinal use champagne. And for a Smoking Pope use a fine burgundy.

- 6 seville oranges
- A few dozen whole cloves (it's Christmas, life is too short to count cloves)
- Up to 1tsp each of ground cinnamon, allspice and mace. A stick of cinnamon is a perfectly acceptable addition too. Don't fret over the exact combination of spices – follow your nose!
- 1 decent-sized piece of fresh ginger root (½ an inch), cut into slices
- 1 bottle (750ml) port (this needs to be ruby port and don't waste your finest vintage on this recipe)
- 1 bottle (750ml) red wine (something fresh and not too tannic. A nice Rhône Valley wine or a new world Syrah would do well)
- 100g or ½ cup sugar, or more to taste

Prick the skin of the oranges with a sharp knife and put a whole clove in each hole. Ideally they should be roasted by an open fire. Failing that, put them in a non-stick deep baking dish and stick them in the oven (150 degrees) for 1-1½ hours. They should be starting to brown with a sticky caramelised mess oozing out. Put all the spices together with a cup of the red wine and the same amount of water into a large pan and boil away for 20 minutes until reduced down and the kitchen is smelling heavenly. Then add the rest of the wine until it is heated and pour over the baked oranges, stirring to get some of the caramelized goodness dissolved. Leave this covered overnight. Next day, remove the oranges, cut in half and squeeze the juice back into the wine mixture. Strain into a fresh pan. Add the bottle of port and gently heat until it starts smoking! Taste it before adding the sugar. Too much sugar removes all the subtlety.

Christmas Cocktails

Cocktails are a relatively modern invention and hence a new addition to Christmas celebrations, but don't let that put you off. With a little imagination, and for far less cash than with champagne, you really set the festive tone alight – quite literally, in the case of one of the cocktails I have for you.

In the spirit (pun intended) of the principles I outlined in the introduction, I'd like to offer you three cocktails whose heritage can be traced back over 2,000 years to a cold night, in a barn, in Jerusalem: *The Goldfinger Babe*, *The Frankincendiary 75* and the *Myrrhtini*. If three kings from the East considered that gold, frankincense and myrrh were the most suitable presents to celebrate the birth of the infant Jesus, who am I to disagree? And if, God forbid, there are any murmurings of discontent on your levels of excess you can look suitably insulted/hurt/horrified (delete as appropriate) and say that you were merely trying to bring Christmas back to its religious roots.

As well as presenting your guests with a choice of three exotic drinks, you can then enjoy gazing down from that most enjoyable viewpoint – the moral high ground.

The Goldfinger Babe

This is named after my lovely wife, Jean. Several years ago, we were sitting in a wonderful bar in China where a young cellist was playing the background music. She did this while sitting on a throne made from artificial red roses. We had to pinch ourselves to remind us that this was communist China. The cocktail menu was similarly extravagant. Jean chose a golden champagne and reclined back on our Roman emperor-style benches. When it arrived, she took her first sip and said, "just tastes like normal champagne to me". Even in the dim sultry light I could see the gold leaf glinting off her teeth. She might have just stepped off the set of the film *Goldfinger*, hence the name of this cocktail that is inspired by that night.

The Goldfinger Babe adds the dimension of excess with 22kt gold and adds an interesting complexity of taste (cinnamon and liquorice to name just a few) to the champagne that was missing from our adventure in China.

Danziger Goldwasser
Champagne

The only important step is to give the bottle of Goldwasser a good shake before you start; this gets all the gold foil back up into suspension. This is best served in a champagne flute because you can see the gold flakes better. Fill a quarter of the glass with Goldwasser and top up with champagne. It's that simple.

The Frankincendiary 75

- A double measure of Sacred Distillery Gin – a unique low pressure distilled gin that contains frankincense
- A single measure of lemon juice – from an actual lemon please, not one of those plastic things!
- A half measure of elderflower cordial
- Champagne
- The metal cap from a champagne bottle (*plaque de muselet*, to give it its proper title)
- A pair of tweezers to lift the *plaque de muselet* in and out of the glass
- A few grains of frankincense resin

Mix the gin, lemon juice and elderflower cordial in a cocktail mixer full of ice cubes and stir vigorously for a minute or less.

Strain the contents into a broad, coupe-style champagne glass and top up with champagne. Away from the glass place the grains of frankincense into the upturned champagne cap and get them smoking with the blow torch using a fine blue flame on a suitably non-flammable surface (not your wife's brand new walnut kitchen work surface). They will start to bubble and melt and then catch fire and release their fragrant smoke. Then lift carefully with tweezers and float on top of the drink. The perfect burning frankincense-themed cocktail. If the smoke is getting too much after the first sip, the champagne cap can be popped out onto a saucer and left to burn to give the room a true Christmas aroma.

The Myrrhtini

The final cocktail of the set is, of course, the Myrrhtini which combines not one, but two ingredients beginning with "Myr." Myrrh is a very aromatic-smelling substance that has a rather bitter taste, like many good cocktail ingredients, but to balance that out I've chosen to pair it with a sweet liqueur that has a lovely intense fruit flavor – crème de myrtille. This is a French liqueur made from myrtille – the French word for blueberry.

- High quality edible myrrh resin
- Gin (fond of Bombay Sapphire, but follow your own nose on this one)
- Crème de myrtille (several choices but Edmond Briottet's liqueurs are highly recommended)
- A few blueberries to garnish

A few weeks ahead of time, add 2 or 3 pieces of edible Myrrh resin to a bottle of gin. Shake every day or so. When it comes close to Christmas, strain or filter the gin to get rid of any bits and rebottle. In keeping with its name, the Myrrhtini should be served in a classic martini glass. Place the gin and glasses in the freezer for about 5-10 minutes. Place a small dribble of Crème de Myrtille in the bottom of the glass, then slowly pour on the gin. Garnish with a few blueberries, either bobbing around on their own or skewered on an antique hat pin for an additional flourish.

Wine

What might seem to be the simplest of choices at Christmas, which wine to serve, is in fact one of the most difficult, especially if you care about wine. It is a tragedy of Greek proportions to serve a superb wine only to have almost full glasses, abandoned after a first taste, sitting on the tablecloth in front of various maiden aunts for the entire dinner. Even worse is when they are thrown into the sink by the same aunts who rate a well-filled dishwashing machine over the merits of a fine 1982 Bordeaux. The only rule is that when it comes to Christmas wines, you need to cut your cloth according to the drinking habits of your guests.

The Christmas Wine Shopping List

It's time to make a few suggestions that will suit everyone from a Russian oligarch to more normal folk.

Lebanese Wines

The best wines in the Middle East come from the Bekaa Valley in Lebanon, where they have been making wine for around 6,000 years! Chateau Musar is the wine that has put Lebanon on the map in the modern era. The red wines, which are the more famous, are a blend of cabernet sauvignon, carignan and cinsault. They are wonderful and big-hearted reds in the style of the grand old wines from the Rhône Valley, and age beautifully. For their quality they are reasonably priced (£30 or so), and make a perfect accompaniment to any Christmas feast. I have even seen allusions to Christmas cake in tasting notes for this wine. Their less well-known whites are excellent too.

The Rhône Valley

Within France I am going to stick my neck out in favour of the Rhône Valley wines, which for me are perfect for Christmas. The 2009 L'Hermitage Rouge, Domaine Jean-Louis Chave will set you back close to £400 and earned 100 points (out of 100) from the famous US critic Robert Parker. Imagine that with Carmina Burana playing loud enough on the hi-fi to drown out all conversation

– Christmas heaven. But don't despair; there are plenty of more reasonable Hermitages from other producers and other years.

The Billionaire Bling Wines

The standard show-off wines are two iconic names in French wine, Chateau Petrus and Le Pin. There is a commonly told tale in the wine trade that Las Vegas sells more bottles of the iconic Chateau Petrus 1982 vintage every year than were ever made in the first place! The buyers are clearly too drunk, too rich or too ignorant to notice the difference between the real thing and the many forgeries or refilled bottles that get sold, but clearly having paid £4,000 for the privilege their brains are tricked into enjoying it or are past caring. You would have to either dearly love your family or be desperate to impress someone to produce Le Pin or Chateau Petrus at Christmas lunch.

The Stratospheric Wines

When it comes to the spectacularly expensive, Le Pin and Petrus don't even make the top ten. One of the consistently rated producers is Domaine de la Romanee-Conti, which will usually take a couple of the top ten slots. They produce an excellent white wine, Montrachet grand cru, which can command a price of several thousand pounds a bottle. This seems cheap only in comparison to their red wine, Côte de Nuits, which is closer to £10,000 for a bottle of the 1978 vintage.

Christmas Breakfast

 Eat a live frog first thing in the morning and nothing worse will happen to you the rest of the day.

Mark Twain

D epending on your age, Christmas morning can start from just after midnight or barely exist at all. Parents of young children will start the day sleep-deprived, and by the time breakfast-time arrives may have been awake for four or five hours. Such unfortunate folk will need both a pick-me-up and an easily prepared breakfast. The party animals who don't have children of their own may wake up so late that Christmas lunch may serve as breakfast, but if they do surface early enough then their needs may be remarkably similar to those poor wrecked parents with the added need for a decent hangover cure. So here are a few simple recipes to get the day off to a fine start and set down a marker that it's going to be an unusual and particularly foodie Christmas.

Dog's Nose

**This drink must be the ultimate
Christmas morning hangover cure.**

It has all the right ingredients: an impeccable heritage straight off
the pages of a Dickens novel, a brilliant name and rich Christmas
flavours. So forget the hair of the dog, if you are feeling rough on
Christmas morning, go for the dog's nose instead.

Dog's Nose is mentioned in Dickens' *The Pickwick Papers* where
it is found, by the committee of the Brick Lane branch of the
United Grand Junction Ebenezer Temperance Association, 'to
be compounded of warm porter, moist sugar, gin, and nutmeg.'
Since he was writing a novel we can forgive Charles for omitting all
mention of quantities so I've included a few measurements which
should act as a rough guide, per person.

Half pint of porter (a type of beer,
in case you didn't know!)
2tsp demerara sugar
50ml (around a double measure)
of London gin
Nutmeg (preferably from an actual nutmeg,
not a jar)
A pinch of mace

In terms of sources of good porter, there are now plenty to choose from.

Fuller's London Porter has a fine reputation and heritage. Others that should be considered if you can find them are: The Famous Taddy Porter from Samuel Smith's Old Brewery, Tadcaster; the wonderfully named Old Engine Oil from the Harviestoun Brewery; and Coffee Porter from Meantime Brewing Company if you need some pretence that this concoction really is suitable for breakfast. As for gin, this should be a London Gin and one with a bit of heritage so I'd suggest Berry Bros. & Rudd's No.3 London Dry Gin. They have been based at No. 3 St James's Street, London, since 1698. I think that is fitting for such a historical drink.

Preparation of a Dog's Nose

Heat around 2/3 of the beer with all the gin and the sugar in a suitably-sized pan until gently steaming and hot to touch but not simmering. Add a pinch of mace while it's heating.

Mace comes from the same fruit as nutmeg (it is an intensely red outer lining of actual nut) and shares much of its flavour, but has a slightly fruitier tang to it. Pour into a tall half-pint glass, leaving space to top up with unheated beer so you can create a bit of head on the drink. Then grate the nutmeg on top of the head for an intense nutmeg aroma and get your Christmas off to a proper Dickensian start.

Scrambled Eggs Roulette

- Toast (this is just a vehicle for the butter and other flavours, so for once good old white sliced bread is perfect)
- Eggs
- Butter (ideally salty)
- Absolutely NO MILK
- Marmite
- Marmalade
- Anchovy relish (eg. Patum Peperium) or chopped tinned anchovies
- Salmon roe
- Smoked salmon
- White truffle (or white truffle oil if your truffle supplier let you down)
- Foie gras (with flakes of salt)
- Parma ham
- Lemon curd
- Ghost pepper (*bhut jolokia*) – world's hottest chilli (or the spiciest thing you can get your hands on).

"Know how to scramble eggs?""

"Oh, you mix them up in a pan and cook them."

"Milk?"

"No thank you, I'm fine."

This at least caused Bloom to turn around and inspect his new student.

"I meant do you add milk to scrambled eggs?"

"Oh, I think you do, don't you?"

"First thing you've learnt at Oxford. Never put milk in scrambled eggs. Destroys them. Salted butter, preferably Welsh, fresh well-beaten eggs, gentle heat. Don't forget the fresher the eggs the more you have to scramble them first. Much thicker white in a fresh egg."

Bloom returned to the alcove and his preparations.

"What's the next thing you'll learn at Oxford?"

"I couldn't begin to imagine, sir."
Eccles was almost relaxing into the situation now, which was developing a charming
Alice in Wonderland tea party feel.
"When to take them off the heat... Do you know that?"
"When they're cooked?"
"Logical enough, but wrong. Just before they are cooked: moist, shiny and mobile but
not slimy. See?"

That was Augustus Bloom, a character from my novel *The Reluctant Cannibals*, explaining to Eccles, one of his students, how to scramble eggs. Augustus is a man who knows his eggs and I couldn't say it better myself.

Once you've followed Augustus's instructions it's time to assemble. Butter the toast first and then cut 9 pointed triangles and trim an inch off the pointed end. With a small cookie cutter, cut a small round piece of toast for the central piece. Arrange the triangles around the centre piece in the manner of a roulette wheel.

Spread or place each topping (i.e. marmalade, Marmite, anchovy relish or chopped anchovies, salmon roe, smoked salmon, white truffle, foie gras, Parma ham, lemon curd) on the triangular pieces, keeping away from the edges. Keep the ghost pepper (or your chosen spicy shocker) for the central circular piece. Then quickly cover the topping with a spoonful of scrambled eggs. Sit back and enjoy the expressions on your nearest and dearest's faces as they play scrambled egg roulette!

Green Sausages,
Square Eggs and
Proper Soldiers

This is a fun one for the younger members of any family or for Dr Seuss fans of any age. If you are invited to a stay for Christmas in a house where there are young children, then this recipe gives the perfect opportunity to give the parents a rest while you are filling the minds of their kids with complete nonsense such as: at Christmas, chickens in Lapland lay special square eggs so they can be easily wrapped as presents.

I came across green sausages in the food hall in Harrods. They were made with spinach and chicken. They looked gloriously out of place amongst the other sausages, and I knew they would be perfect for this book. At a mere £15.95 a kilo, these are clearly no normal sausages. You could probably make your own but it's Christmas, and what would Christmas be without a trip to London and Harrods?

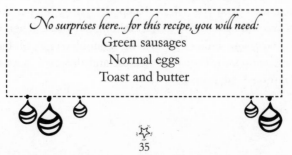

No surprises here... for this recipe, you will need:
Green sausages
Normal eggs
Toast and butter

I'll assume you're happy cooking *sausages* in your preferred way.

Making square dippy *eggs* is a little more challenging, but well worth the effort. The trick is to use a bendy silicone cake mould designed for square cupcakes. Rub the inside of the silicone with a finger dipped in oil so they won't stick. Preboil water in a kettle. Break the eggs into the moulds (so no messy egg shells at the table either) and place into a large shallow pan, then top up with boiling water just to the top of the mould and heat for a minute or two so the egg starts to set then add a little more water to help set the top part. This prevents the eggs going all stringy in the water. Because they are being cooked without the shells but in silicone, the timing changes a little but aim for 4 minutes and adjust accordingly. It is worth doing a few trial runs before the big day to make sure the yolk remains properly runny.

Dippy eggs need *soldiers*. Generations of children have been fobbed off with poorly cut strips of bread and told they are soldiers, but don't soldiers have arms and legs and heads? So butter your toast and get a gingerbread man cutter to cut out proper toast soldiers. The arms, legs and head will be perfect for dipping and, like biting the heads of jelly babies, eating them will give a certain primal satisfaction that you just can't get from a strip of toast. And don't forget to tell them the story about chickens in Lapland laying square eggs at Christmas. Once their parents have survived the onslaught of questions later on, I'm sure they will thank you for firing up their children's imaginations.

Amuse-Bouches, Hors d'oeuvres & Tasty Nibbles

> If the divine creator has taken pains to give us delicious and exquisite things to eat, the least we can do is prepare them well and serve them with ceremony.

Fernand Point

Amuse-bouche is a term that has become popular over the last few decades. Apparently, it sounds more polite than the equivalent term that the French prefer: *amuse-gueule*. These little treats are now de rigueur in top restaurants, but there is nothing to stop you wowing your own guests with exotic morsels as they sip their pre-prandial Frankincendiary 75s or Myrrhtinis. Is there a difference between amuse-bouches and hors d'oeuvres? If there is it is pretty subtle and really comes down to the fact that an amuse-bouche is usually a single wonderful, mind-blowingly good mouthful, whereas hors d'oeuvres don't aspire to such heights. I think of hors d'oeuvres more like pack animals; they are happiest on a plateful of fellow nibbles. Perhaps like a school of fish they feel safety in numbers.

Of the recipes to follow, Rudolph on Rye is definitely an amuse-bouche and the mediaeval mince pies are definitely hors d'oeuvres. As for caviar, perhaps we should call that a canapé or (zakuska, as they say in Moscow). All of which just proves that we have imported far too many words from other languages for what is described perfectly in English as tasty nibbles.

Rudolph on Rye

This dish has an indisputably Christmas theme, though it might cause consternation amongst some once they know what they are eating (or ideally have eaten).

In Lapland and other countries in the extreme north of Europe, the locals take reindeer as much for granted as we do cows. Reindeer provide milk and are used as pack animals. Their fur is used for clothing and shoes. Their antlers are used to make tools and handles for knives. The rest of Europe is slowly catching up. When a certain supermarket offered reindeer steaks for sale in the UK, there were those who objected, but the steaks themselves flew off the shelves in true reindeer style.

Now that reindeer steaks are becoming easier to find, it means that we need to try a little harder to get something truly unusual.

Smoked reindeer heart
Rye bread
Crème fraiche
Fresh dill

The only challenging thing about this dish is getting the smoked reindeer heart. If heading to northern Finland or Sweden in the private jet is out of the question then there is always the Internet. I got mine couriered straight to my home from the Arcticshop.se website. They also have a great range of reindeer-themed gadgets like reindeer antler corkscrews that might be a worthy addition to a Christmas dining table.

Mix some finely chopped dill with crème fraiche and spread a thin layer onto rye bread (ideally Limpa). Place a few thinly cut slices of smoked reindeer heart on top. Serve with a small shot glass filled with Aalborg Jubilæums Akvavit taken straight from the freezer. Since at least some of your guests might find the prospect of eating actual reindeer heart disconcerting, it might be worth describing the dish in Swedish: Varmrökt Renhjärta sounds pleasingly exotic and not at all shocking. Alternatively you could call it Swedish Dim Sum, which may seem a bit of a stretch, but "dim sum" means "touch the heart" so it would have a hint of deceptive honesty about it. This is a dish that for some people might be more pleasurable in the retelling than the eating, along the lines of, "you'll never guess what that maniac next door served up next!".

Once you have put aside all thoughts of what you are eating it really does have a pleasant taste and mouthfeel. It is a very smooth fine textured meat which is firm but also surprisingly tender. The flavour might best be described as a refined mulled bacon which pairs very well with the Akvavit. Without any hints, I doubt anyone will guess what they are eating.

Reindeer Nibbles

If you couldn't get visions of Rudolph out of your mind while reading that last section, or if you are a vegetarian then you can keep the reindeer theme without eating any actual reindeer meat. In the wild, reindeer's favourite nibble is reindeer moss *Cladonia evanii*, which rather confusingly is a lichen not a moss. This would be a far better thing to leave out on Christmas Eve than a carrot, which I'm fairly sure the average reindeer would turn its red nose up at.

The Scandinavians are not a squeamish race and they claim that the best way to get lichen for the dining table is to take it from the stomach of a reindeer just after it has been killed. Even I find that a little odd and the research budget for this book thankfully didn't extend to that. If you think that the more civilised approach of eating lichen picked off a tree still sounds like a Bear Grylls survival technique you'd be quite right, but don't be put off; lichen has started appearing in some of the top restaurants around the world from Heston Blumenthal's The Fat Duck to René Redzepi's Copenhagen restaurant Noma. So why not your dining table?

Lichen, like reindeer moss, can be eaten raw or shallow fried until crispy and sprinkled with crumbled sea salt. This makes for a tasty and moreish nibble to accompany any pre-prandial drink.

Mince Pies

(Just like your great-great-great-great-great-great-great-great-great-great-great-great-great-great-great-great-great grandmother used to make them.)

Back in the 1400s mince pies were being served that had a passing similarity to our modern sweet versions with one significant difference: they contained meat. There is a well-developed urban myth that in mediaeval times strong spices were used to mask the flavour of meat that was getting a bit too close to the edge. It can be tracked back to a book published in the 1930s but is largely discredited. In mediaeval times all spices were brought overland from China along the silk road, the trading routes that stretched from the Orient back to Europe. As a result they were wildly expensive compared to today's prices and serving a heavily spiced dish was a sign of extreme wealth. This means the spices in a mediaeval mince pie would have cost far more than the meat. So it would barely make sense to waste expensive spices on bad meat.

For the Filling:

- 200g Chopped game/meat of your choice
- 100g Suet (finely chopped)
- 1-2 tbsp of Goose fat
- 200g Sultanas
- 200g Raisins
- A decent-sized apple coarsely grated or finely chopped
- A decent-sized quince coarsely grated or finely chopped (a fine traditional fruit that has gone out of favour but is now more easily available. If you can't find any replace with a pear)
- 50g Grated root ginger
- 200g Demerara sugar
- 100g Finely chopped orange and lemon peel
- A small glass of orange juice
- A large pinch each of ground pepper, cinnamon, cloves, mace
- 2 Glasses of brandy (1 for the filling and 1 for the cook)

For the Pastry:

- 170g Plain flour
- 80g Cold unsalted butter
- 20g of Goose fat (cooled in fridge or freezer so it is workable like butter)
- 1tbsp Caster sugar (less than you might normally use as this is a more savoury mince pie)
- 1 Large free-range egg yolk

For an added twist sprinkle the tops with edible pearl dust. If your guests fail to appreciate your efforts, or mutter words such as, "I like those Marks and Spencer ones better", then you can take great pleasure in muttering under your breath, "pearls before swine", before topping up your glass and swigging down some consolatory mead.

43

To make the *perfect mince pies*, first you need to visit your local friendly game butcher and get a few off-cuts of whatever he has on offer. A bit of venison steak would do nicely, perhaps with a little rabbit or hare and a smidgeon of wild boar. Finely chop the meat and soak it in a little brandy, adding a good pinch of salt and the spices. Leave this mixture overnight and the next day brown the meat in goose fat over a medium heat. For a bit of theatricality, feel free to flame off the alcohol during this process. Let it cool down, then add the rest of the brandy and the dried fruit, suet and other ingredients. Combine well. Store in the fridge for at least 24 hours to let the flavours combine.

The next day, cut the butter and goose fat into small cubes. Put the flour into a large bowl with a pinch of salt. Add the butter and fat and rub into the flour with your finger tips until crumbly. Add the sugar and yolk from the egg. Add a little water until it comes together into well-formed dough. Roll into a ball, cover with cling film and put in fridge to cool down.

Take a short break and, after your *well-earned glass of brandy*, roll out the pastry and cut large circles for the base and star shapes for the lids. Put the bases into a well buttered tart tray, fill with the mixture, and put on the lids. Brush tops with a beaten mixture of milk and egg yolk, then bake for 15-20 minutes until golden brown.

Blinis à la Escoffier

Blinis (or perhaps more correctly blini) have acquired a certain kudos in recent years. You can of course buy blinis in the supermarket but that wouldn't do for the sort of Christmas feast that this book is designed to create. Making blinis is not terribly difficult and you can make far nicer ones at home than any you'll buy in a plastic packet. They are also a fabulous way of getting out of some of the more tedious elements of preparation at Christmas, such as wrapping presents - **sorry darling I'd love to help, but I've got sooo many blinis still to make.**

🕯340g plain flour   🕯3/4 pint of milk   🕯15g yeast   🕯2 eggs
🕯1tsp fennel seeds   🕯pinch of salt   🕯1tsp caraway seeds

Warm about 2/3 of the milk until it is tepid; then sift in 2/3 of the flour and mix into a smooth paste. Then add the yeast. Leave in a loosely covered bowl for 2 hours in a warm place.

After this first phase of fermentation, warm the rest of the milk, sift in the rest of the flour, add the yolks of the 2 eggs (keeping the whites aside) and a pinch of salt. Mix this into the first bowl then whisk the egg yolks. Finally whisk the egg whites and add these along with the fennel and caraway seed (coarsely crushed in a pestle and mortar). Leave the mixture for a final 30 minutes of fermentation before cooking. For each blini add 1 teaspoon of batter into a hot pan with a little oil, cooking for around 30 seconds each side until done.

While *caviar* is often served on blinis, I think it is nicer to eat the caviar straight off your mother of pearl spoon and nibble a blini with a little crème fraiche topped with fresh dill to cleanse the palate in between. When it comes to drink, Russia's influence on caviar culture makes ice-cold vodka the ideal accompaniment. While Grey Goose may seem like an obvious choice why not try Zubrówka instead. This is a vodka from Poland that is flavoured with bison grass and has a far more interesting taste than any of the leading vodka brands. It's not wildly expensive but it is rather exotic and outré.

If you want to waste some serious money impressing your guests there is no better (or worse) way of doing this than on ridiculously overpriced vodka to go with your ridiculously overpriced caviar. Imperial collection Fabergé Egg Vodka Gold 75cl does come in a wonderful bottle and the wonderfully high price of £4,000 (sadly my research budget and morals prevented me from tasting this pinnacle of post-tsarist chic). Above this price-point there are plenty of people who have spotted an opportunity to separate the daft-rich from their money. Diva Vodka, to mention just one, boasts a diamond-based purification procedure and the bottle includes a stick filled with gem stones. Does this merit the million dollar price tag? I'll leave that to you to decide, but to my mind it just proves that **the difference between the luxurious and the crass is often a few zeroes on the end of the price.**

How to Roast Your Own Chestnuts (Without an Open Fire)

I blame Nat King Cole and Bing Crosby for a lost generation who think that chestnuts have to be roasted over an open fire and therefore don't try to roast them at home. If I sang the song you'd instantly realise what I mean. It's that classic noel-tide anthem that opens with the immortal line:

"Chestnuts roasting on an open fire".

Freshly roasted chestnuts are one of the best festive nibbles and they appeal to all the senses. They look fabulous. They smell divine. They make wonderful cracking sounds while they cook. The heat in your fingertips as you jiggle them around to cool triggers primal cave-man memories of nights around the fire (or cave-woman; though rarely mentioned I'm sure they must have existed back then too). The lovely tactile process of de-shelling them is a pleasure. Best of all they perfectly capture the taste of Christmases past and are slightly drying on the palate, which brings on a fine thirst for another sip of champagne or your favourite tipple.

Chestnuts are easily found around Christmas time, but it is hard to judge the quality and, sadly, due to the damp British climate, it is not rare to find a few in every bag tainted by mould. Before cooking, the curved surface just needs to be cut open with a sharp knife from the pointy end to the blunt end (otherwise they tend to explode and send hot fragments flying across kitchens at high speeds – you have been warned!). The trick to avoid serving up a manky chestnut is to squeeze both ends after cutting the top and have a sniff, you'll easily be able to detect any mould.

They do need lots of heat but you don't need an open fire or one of those charcoal burners that appear on the streets of London at Christmas. The heat from a kitchen hob is quite sufficient. You can cook them directly on top of a cast iron hob such as an Aga, or on modern hobs use a heavy cast iron frying pan (they can leave burn marks if cooked directly on modern glass hobs). Avoid baking trays as they can warp. Also, don't use anything with a non-stick coating which can easily get damaged by the prolonged dry heat. Heat until the top slit opens up as the chestnut starts to expand and the bottoms are just on the point of charring, around 10-15 minutes depending on the setup you are using.

Serving suggestion:

Best served piping hot to the sound of Nat King Cole.

The Roast Beast & Other Creatures

> A turkey is more occult and awful than all the angels and archangels. In so far as God has partly revealed to us an angelic world, he has partly told us what an angel means. But God has never told us what a turkey means. And if you go and stare at a live turkey for an hour or two, you will find by the end of it that the enigma has rather increased than diminished.

G.K. Chesterton, *All Things Considered.*

The defining dish of Christmas is, in the immortal words of Dr Seuss's Grinch, "The Roast Beast". This naturally leads to the question, which beast?

Should you stick with the Turkey? – a predictable choice, and I might add, a geographically confused one. In Turkey, the bird we call the turkey is called the hindi after India. In France it is 'dinde', and this too is derived from d'Inde – from India. The Portuguese call it the Galinha do Peru (the chicken from Peru), or more commonly just Peru. And in India? Well, there the Turkey is also called a Peru!

You could choose a cockentrice - a bizarre fake creature created by sewing together the front end of a piglet with the rear end of a fowl of your choice. Or a traditional Eskimo dish from Greenland, the kiviak, made from several hundred small seabirds (auks) that are sewn into a seal skin, feathers and all, and left to ferment over the summer. Come the winter the skin is slit open and the locals actually eat these fermented (or rotted) birds.

But enough of that sort of thing and onto the real stuff. Here are several recipes for beasts that will make your Christmas dinner one to remember. Just don't be tempted to create your own kiviak. A few years ago some folk in northern Greenland died of botulism from one. You have been warned!

Turkey à la Pèrigord

We shall start with a turkey recipe, but not just any turkey recipe. Turkey à la Pèrigord is a recipe for one of the most esteemed and rarest creatures in gastronomy – the truffled turkey.

This recipe is based on the one published in 1846 by Charles Elmé Francatelli, a chef to nobility and indeed Queen Victoria. Compared to Mrs Beeton, the most famous author of a Victorian cookbook, Mr Francatelli's name is not well known today. Whereas Mrs Beeton wrote for the rising and aspiring middle classes, Francatelli's *The Modern Cook* was the bible for the stately homes of England and his name seems to have followed their unfortunate demise. One of the most famous lines attributed to, though sadly never written by Mrs Beeton, was

"first catch your hare".

Francatelli's recipe for Turkey à la Pèrigord contains, to my mind, a far better line:

"Have about four pounds of truffles thoroughly washed".

This appeals on so many levels; if the thought of having four pounds of truffles in the larder isn't enough, having someone at your beck and call to wash them ought to be.

For the Main Event:

A fine young (big) hen turkey
About 4lb of black Perigord
truffles (2kg, which will cost
about £1500, should suffice
with a little left over for
scrambled eggs on
Boxing Day)
2lb fatty bacon
Mignionette pepper (a mixture
of cracked black pepper and
white pepper that sometimes
also includes coriander)
Grated nutmeg (Francatelli
is vague about the quantities
here, but elsewhere in his
famous cookbook he uses the
phrase "enough nutmeg to
cover a sixpence" so let's go
with that)
A couple of chopped bay leaves
A sprig of thyme
1 clove of garlic
1/2lb of fresh duck or goose
Foie gras

For the Périgueux Sauce:

A bay leaf
A sprig of thyme
A small chunk of cooked ham
6-8 black truffles
2 glasses of white wine
A similar volume of veal or
chicken stock

Wash your 4lb of truffles, peel and chop into walnut-sized pieces but keep the leftover bits. Place the large truffle pieces into a large casserole dish. Pound the truffle peelings with the chopped bacon using a large pestle and mortar. Add this to the casserole dish along with salt, pepper, a clove of garlic, a chopped bay leaf and thyme. Pound up the foie gras separately and add to the mixture. Put on a very low heat for a hour to melt the fat and start blending the flavours together. Mr Francatelli doesn't add any brandy to this recipe but a good dash of cognac or Armagnac added at the end of this initial cooking wouldn't, in my opinion, go amiss. When done set aside and allow to cool.

In preparing the bird for stuffing Mr Francatelli advises breaking and removing the breast bone. I think this is to make more space for the world's best stuffing, though it might also help the truffle flavour suffuse into the breast meat. He also assumes you are skilled at doing this. If you are not, it might be best to ask your local butcher's assistance. At the end of the day, if that's how Queen Victoria liked her Turkey à la Périgord, that's good enough for me.

Open up the neck skin as far as possible over the breast, then fill up with stuffing. To keep all the precious truffle stuffing in, close up the neck with twine and a trussing needle - there is nothing quite like using a trussing needle to make you feel like you have stepped back in time to the kitchen of one of England's stately homes. The next most important ingredient is time for the truffle aroma to suffuse through the bird. This should be at least 24 hours. A roasting bag, a modern invention not available in Mr Francatelli's time, is perfect for this process as it traps and intensifies the volatile elements of truffles. As an aside this process works wonderfully with uncooked eggs and steak. For eggs simply place your uncooked eggs (in their shells) and a cut truffle in an air-tight container in the fridge until you need them. They will happily soak up the flavour for days. With steak, season with salt, olive oil and chopped truffles and leave for a day before cooking – **there is nothing quite like it.**

For roasting, Mr Francatelli advises covering the bird with bacon and wrapping in parchment paper prior to placing on a spit over an open fire. If you are not blessed with such a kitchen, cooking the turkey in a roasting bag and conventional oven will suffice. Your reward for cooking this fine dish will be being the only person present when you cut into the roasting bag and are enveloped with the **finest aroma known to mankind.**

For the Perigueux sauce, chop the truffles finely and heat in a pan with the 2 glasses of white wine, ham, stock, a bay leaf and thyme until it boils. Bring down to a simmer and remove the ham, bay leaf and thyme. Reduce down and use as the base for making the gravy.

Serve with the best Bordeaux you can afford, and as much *pomp* and *ceremony* as you can muster.

Rôti sans Pareil

Grimod de La Reynière's famous roast without equal requires a degree of skill with the knife and a game supplier with an unusually wide range of stock (and a healthy disregard for the laws of France).

A bustard
A turkey
A goose
A pheasant
A chicken
A duck
A guinea fowl
A teal duck
A woodcock
A partridge
A plover
A lapwing
A quail
A thrush
A lark
An ortolan
A garden warbler

An olive
An anchovy
A caper
A few large onions
A similar amount of carrots,
Chopped ham
A large supply of chestnuts
A forcemeat (i.e. sausage meat)
and bread stuffing
A tablespoon of cloves
A chunk of celery
Mignonette pepper
A few cloves of garlic
Bunches of parsley and thyme
Finely chopped salted pork fat

The birds all need to be deboned. Then start by wrapping the anchovy around the caper and stuffing the garden warbler. For each subsequent bird add some of the chestnuts and stuffing for each layer. Once done place the creation inside a suitably huge and sealable pot along with the vegetables, spices, seasoning and pork fat and cook over a slow fire for 24 hours.

Since most of those birds will be challenging to find, you might find this alternative suggestion appealing. A truly humungous stuffed bird, the True Love Roast, can be obtained in England from Heal Farm in Devon. It costs a mere £670 but that includes delivery and it is dispatched in its own hamper, wrapped in muslin with a meat thermometer in place and sitting in its own baking tray. It will feed over 100 people, weighs 25kg and takes about 10 hours to cook – gas mark 4 (180C) for an hour then 9 hours at gas mark 2 (150C).

A total of forty-eight birds of twelve different species are used in the True Love Roast: turkey, goose, chicken, pheasant, Aylesbury duck, Barbary duck, mallard duck, poussin, guinea fowl, partridge, pigeon and quail. These are combined with a wonderful variety of stuffings: orange and walnut; halzelnut and ginger; juniper; sage and onion; Persian fruit; parsley, lemon and thyme; cranberry and lemon; and cranberry and orange relish.

It takes two people two days just to make the exotic range of stuffings but they can then assemble this monster in around two and a half hours. This is a job that is certainly best left to the experts. In practical terms this must rate as the greatest beast that can grace any Christmas table, provided the table itself can take the weight and you have 100 relatives you'd like to sit around the same table with. Without doubt Heal Farm's creation truly deserves the title of *rôti sans pareil.*

Partridge, Pears and Port

The partridge may not quite qualify as a great beast in size terms, but it is certainly an iconic Christmas bird that features all too rarely on the dining table today. I doubt you can get through the Christmas period without hearing the words,

"on the first day of Christmas my true love gave to me a partridge in a pear tree".

So why not repay your true love by cooking partridges with pears. A few Christmases ago, I bought a butcher's entire stock of partridges on impulse and returned home with little notion of what I was going to do with them. This is the recipe I made up on Christmas morning based on what was in easy reach and made sense at the time. That kind of cooking is always fun even if it doesn't always work, though I think this one really does!

- -
8 partridges   8 ripe pears   1/2 bottle of ruby port
1pint of chicken stock   4tbsp dark cocoa powder
100g butter   2tsp green peppercorns   2tsp juniper berries
2tsp ground arrowroot
- -

Check the partridges for leftover feathers, game birds never seem as well plucked as chickens and turkeys. You can pluck them yourself or follow the example of the French and flame them off with a kitchen blow torch (mind your fingers!). Then season inside and out with salt and freshly ground pepper.

Choose pears with long stalks and peel them while keeping the stalk attached. Cut a bit off the base of each pear so they sit upright and are about the same height as the partridges. Place them in a deep casserole dish. Choose a dish that is just big enough to allow the partridges and pears to cover the base almost completely.

Mix the cocoa powder with about half the port and smooth into the runny paste with a spoon. This is quite a **heady mixture** and **worth a taste.** Then mix in the arrowroot.

In a frying pan, heat half the butter until just starting to brown then reduce the heat and add the partridges (breast down) and cook for 3-4 minutes until the breast is turning brown. Then scoop out the birds into the casserole dish, arranging them artfully with the pears. Leave the partridges breast up and spread the other half of the butter on the breasts.

Add the chocolate mixture, the rest of the port and the stock to the pan that you browned the birds in and heat for a minute or two before adding the peppercorns and juniper berries. Pour this into the casserole taking care not to melt and dislodge the butter on the birds. If you've packed the dish well this amount of liquid should come up to just below the breasts of the partridges and just below the stalk of the pears. Sprinkle the powdered cloves over the birds and exposed bits of the pears.

Put the dish in an oven (around 200C) for 30 mins. Check halfway through and baste the partridges if they are looking dry. At the end, put the casserole dish on a large hotplate and boil the sauce for 2-3 minutes. This will reduce and thicken it into a wonderful glazed sauce. You can add another lump or two of butter at this stage if you wish.

This is a gloriously flavoured dish that goes well with classic game accompaniments such as red cabbage. You could also serve just a single partridge to each guest along with a more traditional turkey if you have guests that feel "Christmas isn't Christmas without turkey". This dish is also perfect for a small Christmas gathering or an intimate Christmas Eve feast.

Goosey-goosey-extravagander

The goose is sometimes considered a posh alternative to the omnipresent turkey. Indeed a roast goose seems to have acquired a whiff of Dickensian tradition, until you actually go back and read *A Christmas Carol*. At the end of Dickens' famous story Scrooge's down-trodden clerk Bob Cratchit sits down with his family for a tasty dinner of roast goose, but Dickens doesn't miss the chance to point out its cheapness.

Bob said he didn't believe there ever was such a goose cooked. Its tenderness and flavour, size and cheapness, were the themes of universal admiration. Eked out by apple-sauce and mashed potatoes, it was a sufficient dinner for the whole family; indeed, as Mrs Cratchit said with great delight (surveying one small atom of a bone upon the dish), they hadn't ate it all at last! Yet every one had had enough, and the youngest Cratchits in particular, were steeped in sage and onion to the eyebrows!

Charles Dickens, *A Christmas Carol*

At the end of *A Christmas Carol*, the transformed Mr Scrooge sends a boy to fetch a turkey as big as the boy himself that he's seen hanging in the local poulterer's and deliver it to the Cratchits' humble abode. **There is no doubt that Dickens rated a good turkey over a goose.**

So far from being posh poultry, back in Dickens' time the goose was distinctly humble fare and enhanced with cheap staples like sage and onion stuffing. That is not to say that a roast goose is not a fine dish, but it needs a little help to bring out its full potential. The fundamental difference between geese and turkeys is that geese are biologically built to migrate long distances and turkeys are, in poultry terms, couch potatoes. This means that geese have to store a lot of energy for their migrations which often take them thousands of miles, and that energy is stored as fat. It also means that the breast muscle is much darker and stronger in flavour.

If you keep both of those facts in mind, it is simple enough to create a recipe that is ideal for a roast goose: the goosey-goosey-extravagander.

A fine goose   250g of steamed chestnuts   250g of stoned dates
Cointreau   A large onion   A palmful of sage leaves
A similar amount of mugwort   A lemon   An orange

The sage and onion stuffing inside Bob Cratchit's goose would have been padded out with bread crumbs, just like cheap modern stuffings. **There'll be none of that kind of cheapness in this dish!** Finely chop the onion and soften in butter for a few minutes then add the zest from the lemon, and chopped dates. Crumble the chestnuts into the mixture along with the chopped sage and mugwort and combine. Add a good glug of Cointreau (100ml or so) and mix in just before taking the mixture off the heat. Stuff the goose from the neck down over the breast and seal up with your trusty trussing needle and kitchen twine.

Season well with salt and lemon. Prick the skin all over with the trussing needle to let the fat escape easily and so that the bird bastes itself as it cooks. Roasting the goose on an elevated rack that fits in a large deep roasting tin is ideal as it allows the bird to roast rather than fry in its own fat. Even with this you will need to decant off the fat several times during cooking. The upside is that you can pour this over the vegetables you are about to roast. Be guided by the timings that come with the goose but for a 5kg bird you will need 3-3.5 hours. The usual sequence of starting off with a hot oven for 30 mins and then reducing down works as well for goose as it does for turkey.

Gravy and Choice of Wine

When making the gravy from the roasting pan add the juice of the zested lemon and the orange. Then chop the orange rind into fine pieces and add that to the gravy while it is reducing down. If it is veering too far towards the sharp end of the spectrum, add a little port or sweet Madeira. **If it's fine as it is, treat yourself to the port or Madeira.**

A crisp wine with a lot of acidity is an ideal companion for goose as it helps to cut through all that goose fat. You might consider: a New Zealand *Sauvignon Blanc*, a *French Vouvray* or a dry *Alsace* wine. Of course, the ideal accompaniment would be champagne, a drink that poor Bob Cratchit probably never tasted.

Dickens eat your heart out!

The Mythical Ortolan

This final recipe is more theoretical than practical and involves a creature whose stature in gastronomical terms is vastly greater than its actual size – **the ortolan in the wild is barely larger than a robin.** The ortolan is also known as the fig-pecker and has a culinary heritage that extends back to Roman times but it is in France that it has retained a mythical status even to this day, a reputation that was only enhanced when it was made illegal to serve ortolan in restaurants because of its endangered status. That didn't stop Francois Mitterand, the former French president, dining on ortalan as he approached death. There are stories of French chefs gathering in clandestine late night meals to follow in Mitterand's footsteps, but unless the numbers of ortolan in the wild recover spectacularly or some ex-banker grows tired of his Scottish salmon farm and decides to breed them, this dish is likely to be entirely off the menu for most people.

• •

The classical French method of preparation and consumption is not for the faint-hearted, though the greatest hardships are undoubtedly suffered by these small creatures. The technique of eating them also has elements of a Hell's Angels initiation rite.

These little birds are captured alive and then fed on a diet of millet (sometimes supplemented with grapes and figs) until they are around four times their normal girth. During this time they are either kept in the dark, or even more cruelly blinded. When it is time to cook them they are drowned in Armagnac, which if I were an ortolan, I might regard as a blessed release.

The preparation is simple. Pluck them and singe off residual feather fragments. Remove the feet and then season lightly and roast (innards and all) for around 7 minutes in a very hot oven. Once ready, place the whole bird in your mouth and bite off the head (that's the Hell's Angels bit) and let it fall on the plate. Once the fat has finished oozing down your gullet, start to crunch the creature, bones and all. It apparently takes a good while to finish munching your way through all the flesh, bones, intestines and Armagnac-filled lungs. Since it must be impossible to speak for these 5-10 minutes, this might be a *perfect* dish to silence a particularly talkative and irksome relative.

The curious French method of eating ortolan is made even more bizarre by the tradition of placing a cloth over one's head during the process. There are various explanations for this. The most common is so that none of the exotic gamey aromas are lost. The more practical reason is that it is such a messy and frankly gross process; I doubt many people would look their best eating an ortolan with their mouth stuffed and fat running down their chin. The last explanation is that the cloth hides the shame of the diner from God. This would seem appropriate if you have been involved in the blinding of the ortolans, though rather deluded since I doubt God would be fooled by a mere teacloth!

Vegetables with a Difference

> ❝ I appreciate the potato only as a protection against famine,
> except for that I know of nothing more eminently tasteless.

Jean Anthelme Brillat-Savarin, *La Physiologie du Goût*

In spicing up Christmas vegetables, let's go for **quality** over **quantity** and **novelty** over **predictability**. So which ones will make the grade? Potatoes are as much a part of Christmas as party hats and crackers so they make an appearance in two guises, despite the reservations of the great Brillat-Savarin about their taste. The poor man would undoubtedly turn in his grave if he knew how many millions of tonnes of French fries have been served world-wide.

Instead of roasted carrots or parsnips why not replace these with something you might not cook everyday. I have always been surprised that the Jerusalem artichoke (and yes, they don't come from Jerusalem either!) doesn't make a regular appearance at Christmas, even just on the basis of its name. As well as celebrating the region where Christ was born there is also plenty of scope for devilment with Jerusalem artichokes so they have made my list. The final selection is a recipe for red cabbage, port and pomegranate seeds which is a wonderful accompaniment for the gamier roast like goose.

You may have noticed that I've dispensed with Brussels sprouts (another food name that doesn't describe the actual place of origin - they were used in Italy in the time of ancient Rome). Personally I'm not a fan of the boiled sprout even when covered with a carpet of flaked almonds and a sea of butter, which to my mind is the only way of making them edible. Before the sprout liberation front start sending me hate mail let me reassure them that while I may have banished them from the vegetable list I haven't forgotten them. In fact I've promoted them. They will appear, Lazarus-like, with coffee in a surprising new guise.

Christmas Potatoes

" *The potato belongs to the family of the Solanaceae... The whole of the family are suspicious; a great number are narcotic, and many are deleterious.*
Mrs Isabella Beeton, *The Book Of Household Management*

Recipes for potato dishes are often not overly complex. Top of the ingredients is, of course, the potato, and in most cases that's all that's said. No mention is made that there are hundreds of varieties of potato.

The most expensive potato variety is *La Bonnette*. This is the only potato I know of for which the taste is attributed to the nature of the soil. This idea is well entrenched with wine and captured in that wonderful word *terroir*, which means so much more than the English word "soil", but is novel in the world of root vegetables. The small annual harvest and the esteem it is held in by French gourmets means that it is wildly expensive (up to £100/kilo). This turns the tables on that well-worn phrase – as cheap as chips (or in this case French fries). On taste and price, La Bonnette would certainly make for the ideal potato for our over-the-top Christmas lunch but only if we changed the date to May when these precious tubers are hand-picked from the ground. The French, being French, do have a special festival to celebrate La Bonnette during this time, but they have to look elsewhere for their Christmas spud – as do we.

Various other varieties of potato have their supporters, but I find myself as intrigued by the names of some of the varieties as their culinary properties. My favourite is the *Lady Balfour*. The lady herself, Eve Balfour, deserves far more recognition than she gets as the person who gave birth to the organic farming movement, publishing her classic book *The Living Soil* in 1943. Today she lives on as a potato, though I wonder what Lady Balfour would think of being described as having pale, tasty flesh. She might quite like the references to creamy-coloured skin, though I'm sure few women would like to be remembered for having a round oval shape.

Beyond Lady Balfour, the English aristocracy seem rather over-represented in the vegetable aisle. King Edward appears twice, once in his normal colour and once in a red jacket. The Duke of York wasn't a man to be outdone by anyone, king or no king, so he followed suit, adding a thoroughly modern pink jacket as well as a red one. There is a nod to Queen Elizabeth from the Balmoral variety and, of course, The British Queen. Lord Rosebery and Lady Christl are rarer visitors, as are the Ulster Prince and Purple Majesty (which might be particularly suitable for Christmas at the home of the artist formerly known as Prince).

The Ultimate Roast Potato

Potatoes
Groundnut oil, or
olive oil, or goose fat
23kt edible gold leaf
Practice
Patience

There aren't many variables when it comes to roasting potatoes so it is surprising how many words have been written on the subject. Here is a simple guide to their preparation:

🏮 Choose your potato, be it aristocratic, musical (eg. The Chopin) or one of the more plebeian roasters (Maris Piper, Yukon Gold).

Different varieties do cook at different rates so a common mistake is to choose some exotic variety you've never used before and cook them for the first time on Christmas morning. That's a recipe for disaster!

🏮 Parboil the potatoes.

After at least 5 and no more than 10 minutes, drain the water and put a lid on the pan. Holding the lid firmly in place, shake the pan so the potatoes get bashed around. This strange procedure fluffs up the starch in the outer layer of the potato so that the hot fat in the roasting tin can produce a well-browned, crunchy outer crust.

🏮 Put the potatoes into pre-heated fat of your choice.

The next step ensures truly golden roast potatoes. Chop the edible gold leaf into fine pieces and sprinkle over the potatoes. It usually comes between pieces of tissue paper and is best cut with scissors while still wrapped in paper. I had tried adding the chopped pieces at the shaking stage but you end up with as much gold leaf stuck to the pan as the potatoes, which is a dreadful waste. Then crush sea salt flakes between your fingers over the top.

Nothing dictates the flavour of a roast potato as much as the fat it is roasted in. Goose fat is a brilliant choice if you like geese, but it's not everyone's cup of tea (to mix a culinary metaphor). Olive oil is very à la mode. It works wonderfully but pulls the flavour in a specific direction. A very neutral oil that copes well with high temperature is the only thing that makes a roast potato taste like a potato, and groundnut oil gets my vote. The most important thing is that the fat is really hot when the potatoes go in and that you roll them around so they are fully coated right at the start.

🏰 Roast for 45 mins (or so depending on your variety)

🏰 The final ingredient is patience.

Try to resist the urge to talk about the real gold in the potatoes ahead of time. Wait until they arrive at the table. It might even take until they reach the plate before anyone notices the gold. Once they do you can nonchalantly say:

"Gold? Of course I put gold in my roast potatoes... Doesn't everyone these days?"

Truffle and Potato Snow

For the first part of this dish you need only follow the instruction of Mrs Beeton.

Choose large white potatoes, as free from spots as possible; boil them in their skins in salt and water until perfectly tender; drain and dry them thoroughly by the side of the fire, and peel them. Put a hot dish before the fire, rub the potatoes through a coarse sieve on to this dish; do not touch them afterwards, or the flakes will fall, and serve as hot as possible.

To turn this snow into a dish fit for an emperor you need to alternate layers of hot potato snow with grated fresh white truffle. This king of fungi is easily affected by heat and so not well suited to cooking. Shaving or grating onto hot food is considered the ideal way of serving white truffles. This provides enough heat to release all the volatile flavours without destroying them.

Potatoes

Salt

1 medium sized white truffle

As well as fine champagne, rappers are also developing a taste for white truffles. New York chef Daniel Boulud has been reported as saying that P-Diddy (aka Puff Daddy/Sean Combs) requests a little more white truffle on his plate with the immortal words, "shave this b*tch". Just in case any young children or mother-in-laws are listening during the preparation of this dish, I suggest you don't follow his example.

Jerusalem Artichokes

When it comes to badly-named vegetables, the Jerusalem artichoke wins hands down – they are not true artichokes and come from North America not Jerusalem. Botanically they are closer to the sunflower, but were linked to real artichokes by Samuel de Champlain in 1605 when he tasted some and judged their flavour to be reminiscent of the European artichoke. As for the Jerusalem bit this appears less certain. One theory is that it is a corruption of the name of a Dutch town where they were first commercialised in Europe – Ter Neusen – presumably by someone who was half-deaf, half-drunk and had a speech impediment. But leaving that aside, since Christmas is all about celebrating the birth of Jesus in Bethlehem, which is less than 6 miles away from Jerusalem, they seem to me to be the perfect Christmas vegetable.

The simplest and best way to cook Jerusalem artichokes is to bake them in their skins. They have a high sugar content so will caramelise naturally in the oven. Jerusalem artichokes are, despite their name, a root vegetable, and are quite variable in size and appearance. The smallest tubers can look rather maggot-like. The similarly tasting Chinese artichokes look even more like bugs. If you can find these varieties then you can gross out your more squeamish guests by telling them they really are maggots.

Groundnut oil
Sea salt flakes
Walnut oil
Chopped parsley for serving
Whole small Jerusalem
artichokes (or larger ones
chopped in pieces)

Rather then peel them (which is fiddly for the small ones) scrub them with a mushroom-cleaning brush (or clean kitchen scrubber if your kitchen gadget drawer isn't so well endowed).

Place in a baking dish and coat well with groundnut oil. Sprinkle with crumbled flakes of sea salt. Bake for 30 minutes at 180-190C for small ones and up to 45 minutes for larger ones.

To serve, season with pepper, a dash of walnut oil (to bring out their nutty flavour) and a sprinkle of parsley.

A Sting in the Tail

This vegetable has many loyal fans but has made more than a few enemies from those who try it, and people who sit next to those people on the bus. This is a case where every silver lining has a cloud – in this case of a noxious variety. Rather than being full of starch, the Jerusalem artichoke stores most of its energy as inulin (nothing to do with the similar sounding insulin), which we humans can't digest. This makes it low in calories but has the side effect that bugs in our intestines have a field day and celebrate by turning all that lovely inulin into gas. It is not for nothing that they are sometimes called fartichokes.

Red Cabbage, Port and Pomegranate

Red cabbage doesn't appear very often on the typical dining table but is a great choice at Christmas on the basis of its vibrant red colour and its flavour. This recipe turns a boring cabbage into a Cinderella with a flowing red velvet ball gown. Well, it doesn't really but you get the drift.
This is seriously posh cabbage.

1 whole red cabbage
1 large eating apple
(cored and chopped)
2 heaped tbsp of whole
fresh cranberries
1 chopped onion (can be a
red onion but by the end of
cooking, everything
in this dish is red so it
really doesn't matter!)
200ml of ruby port
1tbsp of red wine vinegar
A pinch of ground mace,
cinnamon and ground cloves
Seeds from a large
pomegranate
1 blood orange

Finely slice the cabbage. Put a large knob of butter in a casserole dish and place on the hob on low heat. Add the chopped apple and onion and stir to coat well. After a few minutes add the cabbage, cranberries, port, spices, and vinegar. Season well. You can use supermarket red wine vinegar but apart from colour it has little in common with wine! Bring everything up to a simmer and put a lid on. Leave in a low oven for 2 hours. To serve, place in a dish with a ring of blood orange slices around the rim and sprinkle the pomegranate seeds over the top to make one of the best looking cabbage dishes you'll ever see.

Christmas Puddings

 Custard: A detestable substance produced by a malevolent conspiracy of the hen, the cow, and the cook.

Ambrose Bierce, *The Enlarged Devil's Dictionary*, 1911

E very Christmas needs a pudding and every pudding needs a topping. That might be cream, brandy butter or custard, a substance that is loved in Britain and treated with a certain suspicion in other countries. What is even more surprising is that the British affection for custard is based on a culinary lie of staggering proportions. In 1837, Alfred Bird invented a mixture of cornflour starch, sugar, a little salt and the yellow food dye annatto. Alfred's wife was allergic to eggs, and he created this mixture as the world's first egg-free custard powder. It was an invention that made him a very rich man as well as pleasing his wife. So while Bird's custard powder may not be a recipe for real custard it proved to be a recipe for a very happy marriage.

I, as many of you probably were, was brought up on Bird's custard and loved it. Until I tasted the real thing that is. So if you are putting custard on your plum pudding (and there is no shame in that) make sure it is real custard, one good enough to make Ambrose Bierce eat his words. The recipe in this section for duck egg and amaretto custard should fit the bill.

In getting evangelical about real custard I am guilty of putting the cart before the horse. Let's not forget the pudding itself. There are so many recipes for Christmas pudding it is a challenge to break new ground, but I hope my Christmas plum and chocolate bomb hits the mark. To add a little extra drama I turn to science to make the wispy blue flames of brandy more exciting and raid the wine cellar in search of the perfect dessert wine. As a final flourish let's turn your taste buds upside down and inside out (but only for a while!).

The curious thing about traditional Christmas pudding is that it is called a plum pudding yet most recipes don't contain plums, even Mrs Beeton's recipe for an "Unrivalled Plum-Pudding" that inspired this one. Once dried, the appetising sounding plum turns into the far less inspiring-sounding prune, but chopped up in Christmas pudding the much maligned prune can finally achieve greatness. The other thing that is missing from Christmas pudding is chocolate. So let's put both of those things right.

The Christmas Plum and Chocolate Bomb

For the Pudding

125g muscatel raisins
125g currants
125g sultanas
125g chopped, pitted prunes
250g soft brown sugar
250g bread crumbs
250g finely chopped suet
4 eggs
A handful of mixed candied peel
Rind of half a lemon
1 tsp nutmeg
1 tsp ground cinnamon
75ml brandy
75ml Madeira

For the Chocolate Ganache Centre

Fine dark chocolate (Pralus's pure Indonesian criollo, if obtainable. The amount depends on the size of your ice ball mould, you'll need enough to half fill the mould. If you have too much, don't worry, it won't last long.)
Double cream (equal weight to the chocolate)
A dash of green chartreuse

Mix all the dry ingredients in a large bowl. Then beat the eggs and strain into the mixture (this keeps out any stringy bits of egg white) with the brandy and Madeira. Mix thoroughly.

To make the centre of the pudding, melt the chocolate in a bowl suspended in a pan over simmering water. Once soft, melt in a knob of butter, a good dash of green chartreuse and mix in the cream. Then put this mixture in a piping bag and pipe into a silicone mould for making spherical ice balls and place into the freezer to solidify.

This pudding needs to be spherical. Ball-shaped pudding moulds are now easy enough to find in specialist kitchen shops or online. Once the chocolate centre is solid, you can start assembling the final pudding. Butter the inside of the mould, fill both sides and push firmly into place. Then scoop out a hole in the centre of each half, big enough for the chocolate ball to sit in. Finally, peel off the silicone mould from the chocolate, and push the ball into the hole in one side and seal up the pudding mould. It can be stored for a few days in the fridge, but with the fresh cream it probably shouldn't be left for months like many Christmas puddings. It will need a good 6 hours of steaming in a closed pan to cook. It is best cooked the day before and then reheated on Christmas day (an hour should do). Test with a skewer to make sure the chocolate centre is molten before serving.

When serving, make the most of the bomb idea with the addition of a small sparkler. As a final flourish combine that with the salted brandy (to follow) for far more impressive flames.

If this doesn't impress your guests, nothing will!

Salted Brandy

Salted caramels and bars of chocolate with flakes of salt are becoming much more common these days. We are going to add a flourish to our Christmas pudding by using salted brandy. The problem with burning brandy is that the flames are such a faint blue that the dramatic impact is often underwhelming. Table salt contains sodium, which when it burns, produces an intense yellow flame. By combining salt with brandy we are getting both the *salty-sweet vibe* and more impressive *yellow flames.*

Add a large pinch of salt to a small glass of brandy and mix well to dissolve. Pouring it over the hot pudding and lighting sometimes doesn't work quite as well as heating the brandy in one of those tiny little pans you'll see in kitchen shops these days, lighting it in the pan and then pouring it over the pudding. At the start it is the volatile alcohol vapours which burn off but as the flames lick the side of the salty brandy-soaked pudding, they will get even more yellow.

P.S. Light the sparkler on the Christmas bomb first or you'll have burnt hands!

P.P.S. Burning brandy on our Christmas puddings has an interesting resonance as it relates to why brandy is called brandy in the first place. Brandy used to be called "brandy wine" from the Dutch word brandewijn which literally means burnt wine!

Duck Egg Custard with Amaretto

Let's banish the Bird's and make a very special version of the real thing! Amaretto is an almond-based liqueur which brings a very Christmassy flavour to the custard and the duck eggs make for a very special rich custard with not a speck of E160b in sight.

275ml milk
275ml single cream
50g caster sugar
5 duck eggs
(only the yolks)
1 vanilla pod
1tbsp amaretto

Warm the milk and cream in a pan. Slice open the vanilla pod and, with the back of the knife, put the tiny seeds into the milk along with the whole pod. Keep on a low heat for 10 minutes but don't let it boil.

Mix the egg yolks and sugar in a large bowl. Then slowly add the milk and cream to the eggs, stirring continuously. Once fully mixed return to the pan and continue on a low heat, stirring until thickened.

Take care not to overheat; you are making custard not scrambled eggs! You can scoop out the vanilla pod near the end and add the amaretto just as it's reaching the right consistency and you are starting to feel **extremely smug** and superior for making the **world's best custard**.

If you are starting to panic about your custard being too runny, and perhaps blaming the unusually small yolks of your ducks' eggs, you can stir in another yolk or just add a little cornflour mixed into a paste with cold milk. **If you are on your own, no one will know!**

Dessert Wines

Intensely rich and sweet desserts like this can overpower most wines and Christmas is the perfect time to serve a dessert wine. In the spirit of these recipes, this is no time for the mundane or predictable – go for the best and most unusual.

Chateau D'Yquem

The empress of dessert wines is Chateau D'Yquem, the classic Sauternes from Bordeaux. This style of wine is made from grapes that are left to shrivel on the vine as they are infected with a type of fungus called botrytis that causes a condition the French call *pourriture noble* or "noble rot". As off-putting as that sounds it produces extraordinarily rich and complicated sweet wines like Chateau D'Yquem. This wine lasts for decades (indeed centuries) in the bottle, getting steadily more complicated and expensive. In 2011 a bottle of 1811 D'Yquem sold for £75,000. Remarkably, even at 200 years old it should still be quite drinkable. For the less extravagant, a bottle from one of the better years of the last century will cost you only a few thousand pounds.

Maury and Banyuls

This style of wine was developed in the thirteenth century by an alchemist, Arnaldus de Villa Nova, and is only made in a few towns at the foot of the Pyrenees. These two wines are both red dessert wines that are made in a unique way: distilled grape spirit is added during the early fermentation of the grapes, stopping the process while the sweetness of the fruit remains. These two wines are therefore fortified wines like port but have a very distinctive flavour and are an excellent match for Christmas pudding. Impressively vintages such as a 1929 Maury can be obtained for £100-200, a positive bargain compared to D'Yquem.

This is a dish for the adventurous and brave. You don't need to make very much of this dish, the **wow factor** comes in **two spoonfuls!** It is also a dish that should only be served once all the best wines have been drunk (for reasons that will be explained), so it makes a great finale for your feast.

Balsamic Vinegar Sorbet and Miracle Frooties

220g white sugar

125ml water

375ml of balsamic vinegar (use the normal runny type)

A few tablespoons of vodka, or a large dash if you can't be bothered measuring it!

Miracle fruit extract (such as Miracle Frooties, which amazingly are now available from Amazon, or head down in the private jet to Mali in West Africa to get some fresh ones).

Prep: Put the water and sugar in a pan. Warm gently while stirring to dissolve all the sugar. Take off the heat and add the vinegar. Let this mixture fully cool before adding the vodka. Turning this liquid into sorbet requires freezing, ideally using an ice-cream maker. The vodka helps this process by reducing the freezing temperature of the mixture and making for a softer sorbet. It can be made without an ice-cream maker by putting it in a shallow dish and taking it out of the freezer every 15 minutes or so for a vigorous stir until frozen.

Serving: This is a dish that requires instructions for your guests. The sorbet should be served in small glasses placed on a plate. In Alice in Wonderland style put the miracle fruit tablets in small envelopes that are used for labelling gifts and write "eat me" on the outside of the envelope. Ask your guests to try the sorbet which, even with all the sugar, will taste pretty awful. Then ask them to suck (not swallow) the bland tasting miracle fruit tablets for a minute or two. They can then try the sorbet again. It will be transformed into a curious, but very enjoyable and intensely sweet sorbet.

Miracle fruit, as its name suggests, is a very unusual type of food. It contains a compound, miraculin, that changes how our taste buds operate for thirty minutes or so. After eating miracle fruit (or the extract in tablet form), sour foods like vinegar or lemon juice taste intensely sweet without affecting our ability to enjoy other tastes. After trying miracle fruit it is also worth taking the last sip from your glass of champagne or white wine. It will taste dire, proof of how much we underestimate acidity as an essential part of a wine's flavour.

P.S. If you like conspiracy theories, look up what happened in the 1970's when a company called Miralin tried to bring miracle fruit extracts to the market as a dieting aid, allowing people to get their sweet fix without the calories of sugar. In brief, it involves the story of how a young Donald Rumsfeld allegedly manipulated the US FDA (Food and Drug Administration) to block miracle fruit being used in food products while reversing an initial ban on the artificial sweetener aspartame. It makes fascinating reading, but trust me, NASA really did land on the moon.

Christmas Cheeses

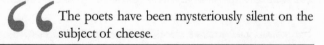

"" The poets have been mysteriously silent on the subject of cheese.

G.K. Chesterton

Cheese is the perfect end to a day of extreme over-indulgence. The Christmas feast should be regarded as a whole day of consumption, rather than a single meal, and what better way to finish than beside the glowing embers of a open fire with a plate of fine cheese.

Of all man-made foods nothing quite compares to cheese in terms of the variety of appearance, colour, smell and taste. Cheese makers toil away for months in chilly barns to create all these wonderful cheeses, so it is only a matter of respect to serve it in a way that does them and their creations full credit. To my mind that means banishing the dreaded cheese cracker selection box. By all means buy such abominations as gifts for people you despise, but please don't serve them with cheese! Thick floury crackers will suffocate all the subtle flavours in any cheese. Strongly flavoured crackers will impose their own will on the cheese, like a bit actor trying to steal a scene.

To that end, each of the cheeses in my Christmas selection has been paired with an alternative to the dreaded cracker.

Colston Bassett Stilton

Stilton, the king of cheeses, is a quintessential part of Christmas for reasons that have been lost in time, and last year Colston Basset was crowned the king of kings at the International Cheese Awards. It has a fine creamy taste without the acrid intensity found in some Stiltons. Blue cheeses are particularly good served on thin slices of pear in place of bread or a cracker. A drop of aged balsamic on top works wonders too. In terms of wine pairings forget red wine, blue cheeses like stilton work much better with sweet wines such as Sauternes or fortified wines such as port (especially the less commonly found white ports).

Vacherin Mont d'Or

This cheese is my favourite and outrageously rich in flavour. This isn't a traditional Christmas cheese but it really ought to be. You might need a few hours for lunch to digest before tackling one of these beauties. It is sold in small wooden cases and, while it can be eaten cold, it only reaches its true heights when baked.

To prepare, remove any outer plastic wrapping and the lid, make a few small stab incisions in the top of the cheese and slide in finely sliced pieces of garlic and single leaves of rosemary. Put the whole thing in the oven for 10 minutes along with some left over roast potatoes from lunch and chunks of baked ham. To serve cut off the rind on top. Then dip pieces of potato and ham into the molten cheese using forks or fondue skewers – sinfully good!

Juustoleipä – Squeaky Reindeer Cheese

This Finnish speciality is traditionally made from reindeer milk but is commonly made from cow's milk these days. It is unusual in being a baked cheese. The cooking makes for a slightly caramelised outside and a creamy interior – in appearance it resembles French toast which makes sense because in Finnish its name means "bread cheese".

You'll need to fly to Finland to get your hands on the real stuff, but a curious alliance of Finnish settlers in Wisconsin and the local milk marketing has given it a new lease of life in America. It is often served with honey or jam, but to celebrate its rebirth in America and its resemblance to French toast why not try it warmed up, cut into cubes with maple syrup?

Three Moose Cheese

This one is acclaimed as the most expensive cheese in the world and is made by the Älgens Hus (The Elk House) in Bjurholm, Sweden. Three moose cheese is so named because it comes from three moose: Gullan, Haelga, and Juno. Unlike cows, moose only lactate for a short period during the summer so the production is limited to around 300kg a year. After that the laws of supply and demand take over, leading to an alleged price of over £300/kg. In reality you'll probably need to head to Sweden and visit the farm to taste one of their three varieties (a hard cheese, a blue veined cheese and a feta-like cheese). This has the added bonus that you can get to stroke a real moose, which is the best possible accompaniment to this exotic type of cheese – far better than any cracker.

Coffee & Petits Fours

After a good dinner, one can forgive anybody,
even one's own relations.

Oscar Wilde

By this stage in the festivities everyone, including the cook, is starting to mellow out and forgiveness is in plentiful supply, but our feast isn't over yet.

After a fine dinner it is right and proper to linger over coffee, a few petits fours and a glass of something to settle the digestion. Perhaps it is time to settle onto the sofa for a post-prandial movie. This is all the more essential in the modern era. The lack of staff these days means that this time of relaxation and reflection is an important respite between the feast and the fairy liquid.

Once you've decided how to serve your coffee, you'll need to think about what to serve with it. An After Eight mint might do at a normal dining table, but surely not after a meal like this. There is also the moral tale of Mr Creosote from Monty Python's *The Meaning of Life*, who explodes on the back of eating just such a wafer thin mint. If nothing else, that should encourage you to find some more imaginative alternatives to shop-bought chocolates.

This is the final chance to surprise and delight your guests. Don't disappoint them at the last hurdle!

Irish Coffee

Irish coffee harks back to the romantic days of air travel in the late 1930's when shining aluminium seaplanes used to fly into Foynes, off the west coast of Ireland. This era certainly looks glamorous in black and white photographs but a flight from New York took around twenty-four hours so the best part of the journey was probably stepping off the plane. It was Joe Sheridan, one of the chefs at Foynes, who first offered whiskey-laden coffee to cheer up arriving passengers. He quickly developed it into the drink we know today. Served in a glass with the cream floating on top, it was designed to mimic Ireland's other famous drink, Guinness. Over the years a wide range of dreadful concoctions involving cream sprayed from cans have been called "Irish coffee". Whatever that beverage is, it isn't Irish coffee. To make amends for these heresies make a decent Irish coffee this Christmas, in tribute to Joe and those early pioneers of air travel. All it requires is a combination of excellent ingredients with a little understanding of physics.

- -

Good strong coffee
Double cream or whipping cream, very lightly whisked.
Soft brown sugar
Irish whiskey
(strange as it seems, people sometimes get this wrong! If you are buying Irish whiskey specially for this, try a 12 year old Redbreast, or the wonderfully named and great-tasting Writer's Tears).

Physics

Irish coffee requires the cream to float on top of the coffee. This means we need the cream to be lighter than the coffee. So the cream must be high in fat. The problem is that whiskey is less dense than coffee. The more whiskey you add, the harder it is to get the cream to float. Sugar makes coffee a little denser, which is why adding sugar helps – the more whiskey you want in your Irish coffee, the more sugar you'll need to add. The last problem is that coffee and cream are also miscible (easily mixed), unlike oil and water for example. Whipping the cream very lightly so it can still be poured helps to make it a bit stiffer so it won't mix as easily. As an added bonus the air makes it float better. Strictly speaking this is cheating **(real Irish men don't whip their cream)**, but it makes it easier for the occasional Irish coffee maker.

Preparation

Warm a long-stemmed glass with hot water and dry well. Then add the warmed whiskey and hot coffee. The ratio of whiskey to coffee shouldn't exceed 1:2 if you want it not too sweet, your cream to float and your guests to remain upright. That way you can add just 1 teaspoon of soft brown sugar. The original recipe is far more potent and sweeter, calling for 1 measure (in Ireland this is 35ml) of coffee, 1 measure of Irish whiskey and 2 teaspoons of sugar. To create the cream head use the warm spoon you've used to mix in the sugar and hold it upside down just against the surface. Then pour the cream slowly over the back of the spoon. If it sinks, it's too little sugar, too much whiskey and too little practice. Irish coffee is an art form not a drink. It takes a while to master it, but the practising is fun!

Other Exotic Coffees

If all this complexity is a bit too much, why not simply impress your guests with some unusual and expensive varieties of coffee. I think we are all a bit tired of Nespresso coffee these days; it's time to push the boat out.

Kopi luwak

Kopi luwak comes from Indonesia. It was discovered by workers in coffee plantations who weren't allowed to pick and use coffee for their own use. They spotted that local civet cats ate some of the beans and then excreted them intact in their faeces. So they dried and roasted these beans to make coffee. When the Dutch plantation owners found out what was going on and tasted the coffee they were so impressed they started drinking it too! At £40/100g is it worth it? For the taste I am not sure. For the look on your guests faces when they find out, **almost certainly**.

Black Ivory

With some concerns about how kopi luwak is being made these days on commercial farms, it might be worth looking at other coffees that are made by a **similar "process"**. Black Ivory coffee comes from northern Thailand, and in this case, elephants are used to process the arabica beans first. This has the great advantage from a commercial perspective that there are a lot more beans in each pile of elephant poo than in civet poo. Sadly such economies of scale don't affect the price, but at least they donate some of their proceeds to elephant welfare projects. You can order 175g of coffee, a special coffee grinder and coffee maker directly from Black Ivory's makers for approximately £460.

Chocolate Christmas Redux

When I started planning this book, one of my first ideas was to banish the odious Brussels sprout. Then I discovered the invention of the chocolate-covered Brussels sprout, by enterprising Kent farmers John and Mark Harris. Taking that idea a step further, these petits fours are like a sweet encore of your Christmas lunch.

Although coated in chocolate these morsels hark back to the days of dinners in stately mansions up and down the country, when a savoury course would routinely follow dessert.

So even if you don't live in a country mansion, there is no reason your petits fours shouldn't be stately.

Brussels sprouts
Balls of stuffing (of the same size as the peeled sprouts)
Balls of venison sausage meat (again of the same size)
100g each of white chocolate, milk chocolate and dark chocolate
1tsp of finely chopped orange zest
Small pinch of ground pepper and flaked sea salt
1tsp of truffle oil
(and 1tsp of finely chopped black truffles if possible)
2tsp of light cooking oil

The Brussels sprouts need to have the outer layers peeled off and the stalks well trimmed. They are excellent raw, but if you prefer them slightly softer, drop into boiling water for no more than 2-3 minutes, then cool down in cold water and dry. The sulphurous flavour of sprouts comes out more the longer they are cooked, so they still need to be very crunchy.

The sausage meat balls are simply made by cutting open the sausages and making balls by rolling the meat between your palms (cover your hands with flour first). Fry or bake the balls and then let cool. Similarly roll the stuffing into balls, bake and let cool.

Melt the chocolate, one type at a time, in a bowl over barely simmering water. A teaspoon of oil helps to prevent the chocolate going granular and lumpy ("seizing"). For the milk and white chocolate use light cooking oil, for the dark use the truffle oil. Be particularly careful not to overheat the white chocolate, it seizes at a much lower temperature than normal chocolate.

As soon as it starts to melt add the flavourings. Orange zest for the white chocolate, pepper and salt for the milk chocolate and truffle oil/truffles for the dark chocolate. Add less than you think you need and taste before adding more. Once fully molten use wooden cocktail sticks to dip the various centres into the chocolate, then place on greaseproof paper to cool and pull out the cocktail stick.

I'd suggest using the white chocolate and orange for the Brussels sprouts, the pepper/salt milk chocolate for the stuffing and the truffle dark chocolate for the venison sausages. But of course, feel free to **mix** and **match**.

Turkish Delight

Turkish delight does indeed originate from Turkey (to break the trend of everything else named after a country in this book), where it is called "lokum". The "real" Turkish delight that is sold in Turkey is a little too firm for my tastes so this recipe is for a softer, more sensuous version. This recipe still follows the original Turkish invention and does not contain gelatin. If you use gelatin, you are making jelly! A different thing altogether. Also the traditional rose water flavour is great, but for something a little different I've opted for more Christmassy flavours.

400g granulated sugar

200ml water for the sugar

1tbsp lemon juice

65g corn flour (increase a little and cook longer if you prefer a firmer consistency)

1tsp cream of tartar

150ml cold water for the cornflour

½ tsp of red food colouring

½ tsp of green food colouring

1 tbsp of orange blossom water

A few cloves, a stick of cinnamon, a slice of orange peel and a ½ inch piece of peeled root ginger

1tsp of brandy

2tbsp of crème de menthe liqueur

 P.S. You'll definitely need a sugar thermometer to get this right!

Put 400g of granulated sugar into a pan with 200ml of water and the lemon juice. Put a sugar thermometer in at the start and slowly bring to the boil stirring until all the sugar has dissolved. Keep simmering until the temperature has reached 115C then take off the heat. Combine the cream of tartar and cornflour in a bowl and add 150ml of cold water and smooth into a paste with the back of a large spoon. When done, put the sugar syrup pan back on a low heat and add the cold flour and water mixture a spoonful at a time. Stir the flour mixture before every spoonful to stop the flour glooping to the bottom. Mix the flour fully into the sugar syrup before adding the next spoonful. Traditionally the cornflour is heated into a thick paste first, but adding it cold and then heating removes the risks of it going lumpy. Once done, slowly bring back up to a simmer and keep stirring. It will take 40 minutes or so to thicken up and turn a golden colour.

While that is thickening put the cloves, cinnamon stick, orange peel and ginger in a small pan with a cup of water. Boil for 5 minutes and then let it cool to a make a sort of concentrated Christmas herb tea.

Once it is really gloopy turn the heat down and put half into another pan, which will need to be brought up to temperature. Colour 1 pan

with the red food colouring and the other with the green. For the red one, stir in a tablespoon of the herb tea, a tablespoon of orange blossom water and the brandy. For the green one, stir in the crème de menthe. Scoop out each of the mixtures into shallow baking trays lined with lightly oiled cling film. This stuff is really like glue and will stick to almost anything, including non-stick baking trays!

Let cool overnight and then lift out onto a work surface well coated with a mixture of sifted cornflour and icing sugar. Cut into squares and roll in lashings of cornflour and icing sugar. The phrase "Cut into squares" sounds very simple but Turkish Delight does not take kindly to being cut! The trick is to push down in one movement cutting the whole length in one go and then pull apart. Store in a cool dry place using greaseproof paper to separate layers of Turkish delight and cover (but not in an air tight container which can make it go soggy).

With each delicious mouthful, ponder how many of your own relatives you'd betray like Edmund Pevensie does on the promise of an endless supply of Turkish delight. Best served on the sofa while watching *The Lion, the Witch and the Wardrobe*.

Dates

As a final flourish, why not include a selection of the finest dates. They have been enjoyed in the holy land for millennia, but have sadly fallen out of fashion in recent years, probably on the back of the uninspiring boxes that appear on supermarket shelves. They go well with coffee but they are also perfect to nibble with one of the digestifs that follow.

An annual pilgrimage to the food hall in Harrods is one of the best ways to get top notch dates in the UK – a vestige perhaps of Mohamed Al Fayed's tenure. If that's too much of a trek, find a local middle east delicatessen. Here is a brief guide to some of the best varieties:

Anbara: Large dates from Saudia Arabia that are highly prized and highly priced. Soft but dry with lots of rich fruity flesh.

Medjool: One of the more expensive varieties. They are large, sweet, soft and sticky – like a toffee that grows on a tree!

Halawi: These are much smaller and very sweet but also soft. A more cautious person might be reluctant to pick up a whole medjool, so these little beauties might be more tempting.

Thoory: A dry wrinkly date that is particularly popular in Algeria. It's chewier than the Medjool or Halawi varieties, but still bursting with flavour.

Christmas
Digestifs

" No, Sir, claret is the liquor for boys; port, for men;
but he who aspires to be a hero must drink brandy.

Samuel Johnson

A meal like this will take a little digesting and it makes sense to follow the French who know a thing or two about such matters. Here are a few of the world's best digestifs – alcoholic drinks taken after a meal supposedly to aid digestion. While that claim might not be scientifically valid, it is an undeniable gastronomic truth that a glass of brandy or port is the perfect way to end a feast such as this.

A list of all potential after-dinner drinks could fill several volumes, so I shall be selective and choose just a few examples of fortified wines, fine whiskeys and brandies.

Port

If tradition could be captured it would come in a port-shaped bottle.

It seems the origin of the tradition of passing the port to the left has been lost in time, but it has created a few social dilemmas. It is considered terribly bad form to ask for the port if the person next to you fails to pass it on. A solution has emerged to solve such a crisis. The person wanting the port asks the person next to them "Do you know the Bishop of Norwich?" This is a coded reminder to pass the port that all gentlemen (and gentleladies) should be aware of. If it falls on deaf or ignorant ears, it is apparently acceptable to ask if your neighbour's passport is in order!

Port is the world's most famous fortified wine and Christmas without port would, for many people, seem unthinkable. If you're aiming for the spectacular, then cheap port is not on the flight path. Fortified wines, like sweet wines, last for extraordinary lengths of time in the bottle or cask during which time they can mature and develop like the very best wines. This allows the great vintages of the twentieth century (and earlier) to become highly prized and highly expensive.

One of the most expensive bottles of port (Taylor Fladgate Scion 1855 Vintage Tawny Port - around £2000/bottle) is a late-bottled tawny port that comes from two casks that had been closely guarded in a family's cellars. It was only when the last of the family line passed away that they were allowed to be sold. They had been there for 155 years and were in perfect condition. Even more exciting was the realisation that the wine inside came from the original European vines, before they were destroyed by the phylloxera epidemic. This epidemic wiped out most European vines and vineyards had to replant vine stock from America that was naturally resistant.

Even this port has been surpassed in price over the last few years by the rising value of the iconic Quinta do Noval Nacional port of 1963, which is made from a tiny section of the Quinta do Noval's vineyard that survived phylloxera. Not to be outdone by young upstarts like this 1963, Taylor's have announced they will be releasing a 1863 port soon!

Massandra

Massandra is a style of fortified wine that comes from the Crimea, though less well known generally than port it has mythical status in wine circles. It is named after the Massandra vineyard which was established by Tsar Nicholas II. If you want to know what it was like to be a Tsar of Russia, the easiest way may be to shell out £1325 for a bottle of the 1891 Massandra (tucked away in the special vault in Hedonism Wines in Mayfair). The chateau at the Massandra winery is also host to one of the world's most valuable collections. There are over a million bottles by some estimates and the racks include wines from the collections of the last Tsar. When Stalin visited the opulent Massandra Palace he was so impressed he made it his personal *dacha* or summer "cottage". Stalin also preserved the wine collection and moved wine from the former Tsar's other palaces to the Massandra cellars for safe keeping.

Whisky

Whisky is a corruption of the Gaelic phrase *uisce beatha*, which literally means: **Water of life.** Ireland and Scotland have an unsettled disagreement over who makes real whisky (or whiskey, with an "e" as it is spelled in Ireland). Apart from spelling the major difference is that no peat smoke reaches the barley during the malting part of the process in Ireland. Depending on where you stand on this divide, this either makes Irish whiskey smoother or Scottish whisky more characterful.

Glenfarclas 25-year-old Whisky

Glenfarclas are a small producer of fine Scottish whisky. The great-great grandfather of the current owner bought the Glenfarclas Distillery in 1865 for £511. That would seem like a good investment, since today that wouldn't buy you even a single bottle of their Glenfarclas Family Cask 1963, let alone their most expensive bottles which sell for up to £7,000.

A slightly more accessible but still magnificent option is their *Glenfarclas 30-year-old* at £145. This has been described as the closest thing to Christmas pudding you can drink (thanks in part to its aging in sherry casks) and is a fantastic after-dinner whisky.

Knappogue Castle 1951

To keep the balance it is only right to suggest an exclusive Irish whiskey. They don't get much more exclusive than Knappogue Castle 1951. This whiskey was distilled by the Tullamore distillery which closed in 1954. The American owner of Knappogue Castle, in County Clare, bought the still-full casks. After thirty-six years in sherry casks it was bottled in 1987. It is hard to find now and only available in tiny quantities with prices from £500 to over £1200 a bottle, a stellar price tag to match its stellar reviews.

Brandy – Cognac and Armagnac

Brandy is a spirit distilled from grapes and then matured in wooden casks. This is done in many places around the world, but two regions in France can safely claim to make the world's best brandies – Armagnac and Cognac. Armagnac is the most historic of the French brandies but Cognac has become the better known. Armagnac devotees will also point out that it is made from a greater variety of grapes and subject to a single distillation which helps to retain more character from the fruit. One or other of these brandies have attended every important dinner and state function for hundreds of years. It would be bordering on impertinent not to invite them to your own Christmas celebration.

J. Nismes-Delclou 1918 Armagnac

Our journey stared with an illusion to the Christmas truce at the Battle of Ypres during World War I. What better way to celebrate surviving another Christmas (hoping of course that you did!), than with a bottle of Armagnac from the year in which the Great War came to a close, 1918. J. Nismes-Delclou are the oldest surviving Armagnac producer and their cellars can supply a remarkable range of old vintage Armagnac. The 1918 vintage is a mere £1150 for a 50 cl bottle of smooth, ambrosial, liquid history.

Henri IV Dudognon Cognac

And finally, it would seem fitting to end this book with the most over-the-top and expensive item that might possibly be served at Christmas. Henri IV Dudognon Heritage is aged in barrels for over 100 years and costs £1 million. As fine as the brandy is, it is the bottle that explains most of the price tag. It comes in a gold-plated bottle designed by the jeweller Jose Davos who encrusts each bottle with over 6,000 cut diamonds. Once you've drunk the brandy you will have a very impressive looking candle holder for next Christmas. Now talking of that, whose turn is it to host Christmas lunch next year?

Postscript:

Having completed the writing of this book, I am at liberty to return to my usual daily toil. To that end it seems fitting to give the final word on Christmas books to the incomparable Pelham Grenville Wodehouse, who wrote:

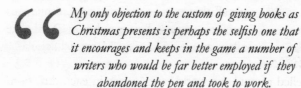

> *My only objection to the custom of giving books as Christmas presents is perhaps the selfish one that it encourages and keeps in the game a number of writers who would be far better employed if they abandoned the pen and took to work.*

P. G. Wodehouse, *Just What I Wanted*, 1915

Although my work is over, yours is just beginning. It's never too early to start planning or saving for Christmas!

Bon appétit and, most of all, have fun!

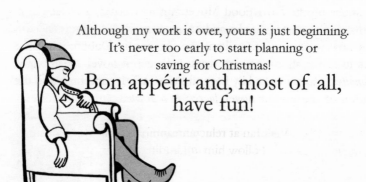

Ian Flitcroft studied medicine at Oxford University, and then went on to complete a D.Phil in Neurophysiology. During these nine years, he started developing a fascination with all things culinary and, on finishing his doctorate, gained dining rights at Pembroke College as a John Lockett Memorial Scholar.

Ian has travelled around the world twice (once in each direction) and sampled many of the world's strangest foods en route from snakes and scorpions, to a soup in Thailand that required all his anatomical knowledge to deduce its contents. Ian is a long-term member of the Slow Food Movement in Ireland, a collector of old culinary-related books and an avid cook and wine collector. Ian now works as a consultant eye surgeon in Dublin, where he has lived for almost twenty years. Ian's debut novel *The Reluctant Cannibals* was published by Legend Press in 2013, and he is also the author of the graphic novel, *Journey by Starlight*.

Visit Ian at reluctantcannibals.com
Follow him @IanFlitcroft

Come and visit us at
www.LegendTimesGroup.com

Follow us
@legend_press